I0442239

TABLE OF CONTENTS

Page

CHAPTER 1

INTRODUCTION

Turkey became a full and equal member of the North Atlantic
Treaty Organization (NATO) in March of 1952. Why did Turkey, a
nation more Asiatic than European, become a member of what started
out essentially as an Atlantic alliance? Is Turkey a reliable and
effective member of NATO? If so, what makes her so?

In an effort to provide answers to the foregoing questions,
this paper examines the geopolitical aspects of Turkey and considers the strengths and weaknesses of the country and its people.

Students of modern Turkey soon learn that knowledge of world
history and the developmental patterns of nations provides little
basis for analyzing contemporary Turkey. The political, social,
and industrial revolutions of the 18th and 19th centuries, which
played such an important role in the development and growth of
Western Europe and America, did not break through the veneer which
held together the weakening and declining Ottoman Empire.

Not until the mid-1920's was Turkey able to break with the
past and make an effort to catch up with the rest of the world.
Since the end of World War I, the Turkish people have undergone an
almost traumatic experience in attempting to make the transformation from the outworn Ottoman Empire to a multi-party Republic.
The attempt by the Turks to modernize their society has required
radical changes in the political, economic, cultural, and social
structures of the country. Therefore, in order to establish an

overall frame of reference for this study, the remainder of this chapter will be devoted to a brief review of Turkey's historical background.

THE OTTOMAN EMPIRE

Most historians agree that the Ottoman Empire came into being during the latter part of the 13th century and that it remained a sovereign entity until after World War I when it was replaced by the Turkish Republic. At its zenith, during the 17th century, the Ottoman dominions included the Balkan Peninsula, the Crimea, Iraq and the western shores of the Persian Gulf, Syria, Palestine, Western Arabia, Egypt, Libya, Tunisia, and Algeria.[1]

The Ottoman Turks were of the Islam faith and accepted the "Cihad," which was the doctrine to extend Islam by force of arms. Islam gave the Turkish state a purpose and meaning but at the same time submerged the national characteristics of the Turks to the extent that "Turk" became synonymous with "Muslim."[2]

The military superiority that was so successful in extending the frontiers of the Ottoman Empire was eventually to be its downfall. The Sultans became content to be Emperors instead of leaders and preferred to remain on their throne in Constantinople and enjoy the fruits of their ancestors' conquests. Also the soldiers,

---

[1]Geoffrey L. Lewis, Turkey, p. 20.
[2]Kemal H. Karpat, Turkey Politics, p. 3.

because of their extended successes, were contemptuous of the West and tended to see non-Muslims as "abject infidels," necessarily inferior to followers of the true faith--Islam.[3]

By the middle of the 17th century, the emerging nations of Western Europe were becoming strong enough to challenge the "Terrible Turks." As these new nations gained political and military strength, more and more pressure was brought to bear on the far-flung outposts of the Ottoman Empire. Starting with their retreat from Vienna in 1686, the Turks suffered an almost unbroken succession of defeats, and by early 19th century the Ottoman Empire was beginning to show symptoms which would later be diagnosed as the "Sick Man of Europe." The defection and ultimate independence of Greece, the successful rebellion of Mohammed Ali, the Viceroy of Egypt, and the destruction of the Turkish fleet at Navarino were indications of the approaching demise of the Ottoman State. The Crimean War (1854-1856) and the Russo-Turkish War (1877-1878) further sapped the national economy and reduced the limits of the Empire.[4]

The end of World War I provided the death-blow for the Ottoman Empire. The army was completely disorganized and ineffective, the economy was in a state of chaos, and the Sultan was unable to govern the areas left under his control. Furthermore, the extent of the Empire had been further drastically reduced by

---

[3]Lewis, op. cit., p. 30.
[4]"Rampart In The Middle East," Army Information Digest, Vol. 7, May 1962, p. 35.

the Treaty of Sevres, which placed the Straits under control of
the victorious Allies; placed Thrace and Smyrna (now Izmir) under
the control of Greece; gave the Dodecanese Islands and Rhodes to
Italy; and placed the Mediterranean seacoast, including Syria,
Palestine, and Mesopotamia under British and French control.[5]

Under these chaotic conditions, the Turkish Nationalist
movement, heretofore limited to a small class of intellectuals,
gained momentum and became forged into a determination to preserve
the integrity and independence of the Turkish homeland. Ataturk
was in the wings waiting to follow what he had long perceived to
be his destiny.

THE ROLE OF ATATURK

Modern Turkey was largely the creation of one man, Mustafa
Kemal Ataturk, whose name still symbolizes leadership, progress,
and national pride to the Turkish people. Although he died more
than a quarter of a century ago, the scowling countenance of
Ataturk is still likely to be the lasting impression today's
visitor carries away from Turkey. Ataturk's photograph peers
from the wall of each business place, and either a photograph or
bust, or both, has a prominent place in every civil and military

---

[5]J. C. Hurewitz, Diplomacy in the Middle East--A Documentary
Record 1914-1956, p. 81.

office. Furthermore, all village squares and the courtyards of the government buildings would seem naked without a suitable statue of Ataturk appropriately inscribed with a quotation from one of his speeches.[6]

Why do the Turks still honor and worship the memory of this man? Primarily, it is because Mustafa Kemal provided the spark and leadership which enabled the Turks to overcome the shame of the defeat they had suffered during World War I and the years immediately thereafter. It was he who, in effect, forced the Turks to rise up and fight until the hated foreigners were driven out of Turkey.

Following the military victory of 1922, Ataturk was successful in negotiating an honorable treaty which enabled Turkey to emerge as an independent, sovereign nation. As the first President of Turkey, Ataturk laid the foundations for modern Turkey and gave political and national content to Turkish unity.

Kemal Ataturk was a reformer. During the sixteen years of his presidency (1923-1938), he instituted reforms which touched on many phases of Turkish life, both private and public. Even today, some of Ataturk's reforms seem drastic, if not completely radical. However, considering the historical background of the Turkish people and the environment of his time, it seems doubtful that any other course of action could have succeeded. Ataturk's

---

[6]Author's personal experience and observation. (NOTE: The author lived in Izmir, Turkey, from March 1962 until August 1964 and traveled extensively throughout the country during that period.)

reforms included the following: the wearing of the fez was forbidden; Turkish women were emancipated and encouraged not to wear the veil; the Gregorian calendar was adopted; Arabic script was replaced by the Latin alphabet; new legal codes were patterned on the Swiss and Italian systems; the sultanate and caliphate were abolished and a secularized constitutional government was formed.[7]

To say that Ataturk's reforms caused a vast change in the lives of the Turkish people is an understatement. The appearance of the people was changed by the forced adoption of western dress, and the social and business relationships were greatly influenced by the modernization of the Turkish language and legal codes. But the greatest changes were made in the area of governmental relationships--both national and international. By abolishing the sultanate and caliphate and forming a secularized constitutional government, Ataturk completely revamped the government, cut Turkey off from its traditional ties in the Middle East, and changed the outward orientation toward Europe and America.

Perhaps Ataturk's greatest achievement was his ability to create the intense nationalism which was required to unify the Turkish people behind a spirit of productive patriotism.[8] Certainly there is little doubt that the strongest unifying factor in modern Turkey stems from the respect the people have for the person and ideals of Mustafa Kemal Ataturk.

---

[7]"Turkey," Encyclopaedia Britannica, Vol. 22, p. 610.
[8]Altemur Kilic, Turkey and the World, p. 49.

CHAPTER 2

FOREIGN POLICY

<u>RELATIONS WITH THE WEST AND THE USSR</u>

Since the middle of the 17th century, the Turks have fought more than a dozen wars with the Russians. All of these battles were the outgrowth of Russia's dreams of capturing and controlling the Turkish Straits in order to insure a free sea passage to the Mediterranean. This extended period of adversity played a major role in the shaping of Turkish foreign policy. Indeed, it is probably true that many Turkish peasants still see the world in terms of two nations--Turkey and Russia.[1] The fact that Turkish mothers still use the word "Russian" to frighten naughty children seems ample proof that the Turkish people remain fully aware of the threat from the north.[2]

From the beginning of the Turkish Republic and throughout his presidency, Ataturk made it clear that Turkey was to be a European state, oriented toward the West, and that France and England, not Russia, were to be his models.[3]

Nevertheless, one of Ataturk's first acts of foreign diplomacy was to make a treaty with Russia. In 1920, finding himself opposed by the Allies and threatened by a Greek invasion, Ataturk sought

---

[1]Geoffrey L. Lewis, Turkey, p. 112.
[2]Claire Sterling, "Turkey's Long Interregnum," The Reporter, Vol. 23, 1 Sep. 1960, p. 25.
[3]Lewis, op. cit., p. 113.

and concluded a military and political alliance with the Soviet Union. This alliance--known as the Treaty of Moscow--was signed in March, 1921, and provided military aid which helped the Turks in their victory over Greece.[4]

In 1925 the Turks and Russians concluded the Treaty of Friendship and Neutrality under which each party agreed to abstain from participation in alliances, coalitions, or hostile actions of any kind directed against the other. This treaty was renewed in 1935 for an additional ten years.[5]

Notwithstanding her agreement and indebtedness to Russia, Turkey soon demonstrated her independence and long-range desire to be associated with the West. During the Straits Convention of the 1923 Lausanne Conference, Turkey joined with the West against Russia in supporting acceptance of the principle of freedom of passage through the Straits.[6]

A tripartite treaty between Great Britain, Turkey, and Iraq, signed on 5 June 1926, lessened the strained Anglo-Turkish relations which had been caused by Turkey's alignment with Germany in the pre-World War I period and with Soviet Russia during the early 1920's.[7] Then, on 18 July 1932, Turkey became a member of the

---

[4]A. N. Dragnich, "A Political and Economic Appraisal of Greece, Turkey, and Yugoslavia," Naval War College Review, Vol. XIII, Feb. 1961, p. 17.

[5]George C. McGhee, "Turkey Joins The West," Foreign Affairs, Vol. 32, Jul. 1954, p. 620.

[6]James T. Shotwell, Turkey At The Straits, p. 113.

[7]Ibid., p. 119.

League of Nations. Ataturk held that this action was in accord with his principle of "Peace at home and peace abroad."[8]

This gradual _rapprochement_ with the Western European Powers led Turkey to the conclusion that it was time to try to improve her position in regard to the Lausanne Treaty. Consequently, in a note dated 10 April 1936, Turkey requested that the Secretary General of the League of Nations call a conference for the purpose of revising the demilitarization clauses of the Straits Convention.[9]

In compliance with Turkey's request, the Montreux Convention of 1936 was called, and the Turks were given increased, although not absolute, control over the Straits. Turkey's position was further strengthened by cancellation of the demilitarization clauses which had been part of the 1923 Straits Convention.[10]

Turkey moved closer to the West when she signed the 1939 Anglo-French-Turkish Treaty at Ankara. This treaty committed Turkey to aid and support England and France in specified military operations in the Mediterranean area, but outside Turkey.[11] However, World War II saw Turkey "sitting on the fence" and trying to maintain a neutral position; she did not declare war on Germany until February 1945. Throughout the war Turkey faithfully observed the provisions of the Montreux Treaty and firmly rejected Soviet offers to participate in the defense of the Straits.[12]

---

[8]Lewis, _op. cit._, p. 121.
[9]Shotwell, _op. cit._, p. 121.
[10]Ibid., p. 124.
[11]Lewis, _op. cit._, p. 116.
[12]Robert S. Monroe, "Geopolitics in Flux at the Turkish Straits," _Military Review_, Vol. XLIII, Sep. 1963, p. 8.

Shortly before the end of World War II Turkey was reminded of the Soviets' true intentions when Stalin denounced the 1925 treaty of Turkish-Soviet friendship, demanded revision of the Montreux Convention, and requested Soviet base rights in the Straits area. He also claimed the eastern provinces of Kars, Artvin, and Ardahan.[13] These demands, which were quickly and firmly rejected by the Turks, revived anti-Russian feeling within Turkey and drove the Turks still closer to the West. Tension between the two countries continued to mount until, by 1947, it was feared that the Soviets might intervene with armed forces. Announcement of the Truman Doctrine in 1947 and the subsequent programs of military and economic aid forestalled the implementation of any plans for armed intervention that the USSR may have had.

Turkey became a charter member of the United Nations by virtue of the fact that she had declared war on Germany prior to the end of World War II. In 1950 Turkey proved her firm belief in collective security by being the first nation, after the United States, to respond to the United Nations' request for help in repelling the North Korean aggression. In announcing that Turkey would send 5,000 men to Korea, the prime minister stated:

> . . . It is only by way of a decision similar to ours, to be arrived at by other freedom loving nations, that acts of aggression can be prevented and world peace can be safeguarded. A sincere attachment to the ideals of the United Nations requires a belief in this basic principle. . . .[14]

---

[13]Claude Desbouquets, "Turkey and Global Strategy," Military Review, Vol. XLI, Jun. 1961, p. 64.

[14]McGhee, op. cit., p. 623.

In 1952 Turkey moved closer to the West by becoming a member of the North Atlantic Treaty Organization (NATO).[15] Subsequently, in 1955 Turkey extended her international responsibilities by joining the Baghdad Pact (now Central Treaty Organization--CENTO) and becoming a link between NATO and CENTO. Although committed to both treaties, Turkey is still basically oriented toward the West and remains a European power strategically and commercially. The principal land, air, and sea links are with Europe, while the mountains, deserts, and salt flats to the east form an effective barrier into Asia. Turkey is destined by geography to be the southern anchor of the NATO defense line.[16]

The military coup in 1960 was the first violent crisis faced by the Turkish Republic. However, the crisis was primarily internal, and General Gursel, the new head of government, immediately reasserted the government's fidelity to Turkey's treaty commitments and pro-Western orientation.[17] The government's intent to stand by the existing foreign policy commitments was further emphasized on 27 May 1960, when the Armed Forces included the following statement in a message to the Turkish nation and the world:

> . . . We are addressing ourselves to our allies, friends, neighbors, and the entire world: Our aim is to remain .

---

[15]NATO, Facts About the North Atlantic Treaty Organization, p. 18.
[16]William H. Hessler, "Turkey--Russia's Gift to NATO," The Reporter, Vol. 5, 2 Oct. 1951, p. 16.
[17]M. Perlmann, "Turkey on the Eve of 1961," Middle Eastern Affairs, Vol. XII, Jan. 1961, p. 6.

> completely loyal to the United Nations Charter and to
> the principle of human rights; the principle of peace
> at home and in the world set by the great Ataturk is
> our flag.
>
> We are loyal to all our alliances and undertakings.
> We believe in NATO and CENTO and we are faithful to
> them. . . .[18]

In 1961 the Army agreed to return control of the government to elected officials and arranged for elections to be held on 15 October. However, the elections failed to give a commanding majority to a single party, and Turkey was faced with a series of coalition governments.

During the period October 1961 to October 1965, the internal situation in Turkey remained in a state of flux while the political parties, nervously watched by the Army, maneuvered for power. An unsuccessful military putsch by a minority element from within the army failed in February 1962. Although this was a dangerous and difficult period for Turkey, it is generally agreed that the problem was internal and that there was no significant change in foreign policy. The fear of the West was not that Turkey would change her foreign policy, but that she might become so weakened by internal problems that she would be more susceptible to Communist pressures.

By October 1965 the multiparty system had stabilized to the extent that the Justice Party was elected with a commanding majority and was able to form a one-party government. The new prime minister

---

[18]Walter F. Weiker, The Turkish Revolution 1960-1961, p. 21.

is considered pro-Western, and there are no indications of any change to the basic foreign policy. The main change seems to be in the direction of more encouragement to free enterprise and of less statism.[19]

One of the most striking developments of Turkey's latest election was the emergence of a vocal, albeit small, Marxist party. Although this party received only three percent of the vote and gained but fifteen seats in Turkey's 450-member Parliament, the fact that it does exist indicates a possible surge of Turkish irritation towards the West. This new party--the Turkish Labor Party--advocates Turkey's withdrawal from Western alliances, removal of all foreign forces, nationalization of the economy, and a neutralist foreign policy. Although this new party must be closely watched, it is encouraging to note that thus far it has been unpopular with the vast majority of the Deputies. When its leader attempted to make a speech denouncing the U.S., he was greeted with cries of "Go to Moscow."[20]

---

[19]"The Change in Turkey," The Washington Post, 23 Oct. 1965, p. A14.

[20]Hedrick Smith, "A Marxist Party Grows in Turkey," New York Times, 16 Nov. 1965, p. 13.

TURKO-GREEK RELATIONS

The Turks and Greeks have been at odds for centuries. At one time Greece was a part of the Ottoman Empire, and ironically enough the great Ataturk was born in Saloniki, Greece, then a part of that empire. Many of the Turks living today, still have vivid memories or, perhaps more correctly, hateful recollections of the Greek invasion of southwest Turkey after World War I. It is interesting to note that during the War of Independence, Ataturk consistently referred to the Greeks as "bastards."[21] Because Mustafa Kemal publicly proclaimed his dislike for the Greeks, it will be a long time before the Turks develop a true spirit of brotherly love toward their Aegean neighbors.

However, in spite of their deep emotional conflict, the Greeks and Turks have on occasion submerged their traditional sensitivities in the face of a common threat. Exposure to the overpowering pressure of communism in the late 1940's brought them together under the umbrella of the Truman Doctrine and American aid programs. The spirit of interdependence was further strengthened in 1952 when both Turkey and Greece became members of NATO and subsequently placed their armed forces under command of the subordinate NATO headquarters at Izmir, Turkey.

Unfortunately, the problem of Cyprus has been a persistent source of fuel for feeding the fires of the emotional conflict

---

[21]Ray Brock, _Ghost on Horseback: The Incredible Ataturk_, p. 219.

between the Greeks and the Turks. This continuing, unhappy situation has weakened the internal stability in both countries and considerably disrupted the joint staff cooperation and military planning for the southern flank of NATO.[22]

The current crisis over Cyprus, now entering its third year, is not so bloody at the moment, but it is as bitter as ever. The Turks still insist on partition and are convinced the mainland Turks will support them if the Greeks try to abolish it. The Greeks still demand majority rule, but for the time being, at least, seem to have adopted a "wait and see" attitude. They may be hoping the Turks will eventually cave in because of frustration, boredom, or poverty.[23]

The Turks suffer a deep sense of disappointment and frustration from what they regard as Western, and particularly American, failure to support the Turkish position on Cyprus. It is not surprising that Greece feels the same way, because the United States was in the predicament of trying to mediate a quarrel between two friends and incurred the wrath of both.

The Cyprus crisis remains fraught with danger. A situation could quickly develop whereby Turkey and Greece could be drawn into a shooting war. Growing conflict or increased tensions in Cyprus can only mean serious problems for the West and a weakened

_____

[22]E. Hinterhoff, "The Strategic Importance of Turkey," Asian Review, Vol. LV, Jan. 1959, p. 55.

[23]Walter Kent, "Cypriot Feud Goes On," Washington Post, 21 Oct. 1965, p. F4.

15

anchor for NATO's defense line. Speaking at the Ninth NATO General Assembly on 19 September 1963, General Lyman L. Lemnitzer viewed the situation as follows:

> . . . Southern Europe constitutes NATO's right flank. NATO's strength in this key area is a major obstacle to any attempt at strategic envelopment of NATO on the South. . . .Our position here would render any Communist offensive against Central Europe seriously vulnerable to a counterblow on its left flank. Similarly, a Communist offensive into the Middle East would leave itself exposed on its right.[24]

The Turkish-Greek situation clearly calls for skillful diplomacy on the part of the United States. It would be tragic if the Americans did not do everything in their power to resolve the problem, or at least to reverse the trend of political development in this key area of the NATO defense line.

---

[24]E. Hinterhoff, "Problems Along NATO's Flanks," *Military Review*, Vol. XLV, Jun. 1965, p. 53.

CHAPTER 3

POWER APPRAISAL

STRATEGIC IMPLICATIONS

Turkey occupies territory in both Europe and Asia. Asiatic
Turkey has about 97 percent of the nation's area--287,500 square
miles--and approximately 90 percent of the population. Somewhat
larger than Texas (267,339 vs. 296,500 square miles[1]), Turkey
stretches roughly 950 miles from east to west and 400 miles from
north to south. The approximately 9,800 square miles of European
Turkey are relatively flat and rolling terrain; the more rugged
terrain of Asiatic Turkey can be divided into three major portions.
These are the high, semi-dry central plain; a surrounding rim of
mountains which become higher and more rugged as they extend into
northeastern Turkey; and a rather narrow coastline on the north,
west, and southwest borders.[2]

Turkey shares a 127-mile land border with Bulgaria, and has a
370-mile land border plus 1,300 miles of Black Sea coast fronting
on the U.S.S.R. Thus, Turkey is in the unique position of sharing
a longer border with the Soviet bloc than any other NATO country.

Located astride the Turkish Straits--the Bosphorus, the Sea
of Marmara, and the Dardanelles--Turkey holds a blocking position

---

[1]New York World-Telegram, "Turkey," The World Almanac 1966,
p. 639.

[2]George B. Cressey, Crossroads: Land and Life in Southwest
Asia, p. 256.

17

which denies Russia the realization of her traditional aspirations in the Near and Middle East. Control of the Straits dominates Russia's strategic and economic communications to and from the Black Sea as well as the most direct land and air routes from Europe to the Middle East and Africa.

For hundreds of years Russian leaders of all regimes have had a primary objective of gaining an outlet from the Black Sea into the Mediterranean. Catherine the Great wanted to establish Constantinople as the capital of a new empire for her nephew. Peter the Great and his successors believed that to dominate Europe and Asia they first had to possess Constantinople and India. Access to warm water--the Eastern Mediterranean and the Persian Gulf--was a preoccupation of the Czars.[3]

On 29 April 1961 Mr. Goedhardt of the Netherlands, Rapporteur of the Defense Committee of the Western European Union, stressed the strategic importance of the Turkish Straits as follows:

> The main objectives of Soviet strategy in the Mediterranean would be . . . the securing of the Turkish Straits and the occupation of Southern European countries. . . . The main threat . . . would come through Bulgaria to Greece and Turkey to try and control the Straits. . . . In any kind of sea war the real threat comes from submarines.[4]

It seems, therefore, that Turkey's principal strategic importance is control of the Straits and, in effect, provision of a

---

[3]Claude Desbocquets, "Turkey and Global Strategy," Military Review, Vol. XLI, Jun. 1961, p. 60.
    [4]E. Hinterhoff, "Problems Along NATO's Flanks," Military Review, Vol. XLV, Jun. 1965, p. 52.

"stopper" which could keep the Russian ships "bottled-up" in the Black Sea. If the Soviets were ever able to control the Straits and enjoy free passage between the Black Sea and the Mediterranean, it would mean the end of Turkey and therefore the loss of the "anchor" for NATO's southern flank.[5]

More than two decades ago, Derwent Whittlesey, a noted political geographer, wrote: "Nowhere on earth have landpower and seapower struggled more intensely or more often than at the double narrows Dardanelles and Bosphorus which mark the ends of the Sea of Marmara."[6]

The geographical importance of the Straits is undiminished today and Turkey remains a truly invaluable strategic asset to the West. In eastern Turkey, the presence of Turkish armed forces near the Russian border precludes a cheap and easy entry into the Middle East by the Soviets.[7]

Turkey is also ideally located to serve as a base of operations. If NATO should have to launch a counteroffensive into the southern flank of a Russian attack into Western Europe, Turkey could be a large unsinkable aircraft carrier from which NATO aircraft could strike Black Sea military and naval installations and the whole industrial region of the Ukraine and Southern Urals.[8]

---

[5]E. Hinterhoff, "The Strategic Importance of Turkey," Asian Review, Vol. LV, Jan. 1959, p. 55.

[6]Robert R. Monroe, "Geopolitics in Flux at the Turkish Straits," Military Review, Vol. XLIII, Sep. 1963, p. 3.

[7]"Ramparts in the Middle East," Army Information Digest, Vol. 7, May 1952, p. 35.

[8]E. Hinterhoff, "Strategic Importance of Turkey," Asian Review, Vol. LV, Jan. 1959, p. 56.

THE PEOPLE

The population of Turkey as of 1 January 1965 was estimated
at slightly more than 32 million.[9] With an annual net population
increase of nearly three percent, one of the largest in the world,
the Turkish population has been increasing at the rate of about
one million people per year.[10] In terms of age distribution the
Turkish population is young; nearly 50 percent of the population
is less than 20 years old, and there are almost seven million
males between the ages of 15 and 49.

The Turks are primarily a homogeneous society, both as to
ethnic grouping and religion. Roughly ten percent of the people
belong to ethnic minorities. The Kurds making up about seven percent and the Arabs accounting for one percent are mostly located
in the remote areas of eastern and southeastern Turkey. The
remaining two percent--Greeks, Circassians, Armenians, Jews, etc.--
are found primarily in the larger cities, particularly Istanbul and
Izmir. Ninety-eight percent of the people are Moslems.[11]

Nearly seventy percent of the Turkish population lives in the
approximately 40,000 small villages scattered throughout Turkey.
In many of the villages, particularly those in the east and the
remote mountain areas, the Turkish peasant's life is much the same
as it was generations ago.[12] These hardy people accept hardship as

---

[9]S. H. Steinberg, "Turkey," The Statesman Yearbook 1965-66,
p. 1485.

[10]Dr. Jurgen Weise, "Turkey and Her Armed Forces," Military
Review, Vol. XLIII, May 1963, p. 81.

[11]Cressey, op. cit., p. 282.

[12]Don Peretz, The Middle East Today, p. 189.

the normal course of events. The wooden plow, the hand sickle,
and the flail are the most commonly used farm implements; the ox,
donkey, or water buffalo usually provides power for farm work and
transportation. In tradition and dress, particularly that of the
women, the Turks remain more Asiatic than European, and their
simple lives are still dominated by age-old customs and super-
stitions.[13]

On the other hand, the traditional Turkish society is changing
rather rapidly in the larger cities. Expanding educational and
employment opportunities have eroded the old taboos and the tight
patriarchal control. Much of this change has come about because
of the increased availability of foreign movies, books, and
periodicals. Also, more and more Turks are listening to foreign
radio broadcasts and coming into direct contact with Americans and
Europeans. As a result of these new influences, the Turks who
live in the large cities are modifying their methods and becoming
more European in their thoughts and actions.

Over sixty percent of the people are illiterate and only
seventy percent of the school-age children manage to find a place
in the crowded schools.[14] The government is aware of this defi-
ciency and is pushing forward to improve the situation. Illiterate
males drafted into the army are taught to read and write before
they begin their actual military training. Also, the shortage of

---

[13]Author's personal knowledge and observation.
[14]"The South-East Flank of NATO," British Survey Main Series,
Vol. 171, Jun. 1963, p. 18.

school teachers is reduced by assigning qualified military inductees to teach school in remote villages. This duty as a teacher is in lieu of military service.[15]

The Turkish society has been unable to provide necessary personnel and facilities for adequate medical care of the population. General Gursel, the incumbent president, has stated that most of the 40,000 small communities, with 18 million inhabitants, have no medical care at all. There are 10,000 hospital beds for tuberculosis cases, but more than 250,000 persons suffer from the disease. Of the 12,000 doctors in Turkey more than fifty percent practice in the five largest cities. The situation has been further complicated by the fact that nearly 1,000 Turkish doctors have emigrated to the United States in recent years.[16]

Although the average Turk is suspicious of all foreigners, more than a dozen wars with Russia over the past 300 years have convinced him that the U.S.S.R. is the principal threat to Turkey's security. Since December 1963 Turkish attitudes toward the Western allies have been somewhat confused by the crisis over Cyprus. While the Turkish people are usually pro-NATO, some Turks have expressed disappointment because they did not receive clear support for the Turkish position in Cyprus.

In sum, Turkey has a vast reserve of underdeveloped human resources. The people have great moral fiber and an intense

---

[15]Author's personal knowledge and observation.
[16]Hans E. Tutsch, From Ankara to Marrakesh, p. 28.

national consciousness. Their future will be determined by the
ability of the Turkish leaders to galvanize those assets into a
major effort in order to complete the transformation begun by
Ataturk in the early days of the republic.[17]

THE ECONOMY

Turkey is essentially an agricultural country with tobacco,
fruit, nuts, and cotton accounting for about 85 percent of her
export trade. Nearly 80 percent of the population derive their
modest income from agriculture, forestry, or fishing.[18] The production of meat and fats is normally adequate for domestic needs
and provides some surplus for export. The cereal and food grain
production is generally adequate except in poor crop years, when
grains and cereals must be imported.

With a per capita income of about $195 per year, Turkey is
one of the poorer nations of the world.[19] The situation is made
still worse by the fact that most of the wealth is concentrated in
the hands of a very few people. Unemployment is a continuing
problem. Even during harvest time 1,300,000 people, ten percent
of the working population, are unemployed. A half million peasant
families have no land of their own, and a third of all farms are
too small to sustain a family.[20]

---

[17]Don Peretz, op. cit., p. 189.
[18]Sir Reader Ballard, ed., "Turkey," The Middle East, p. 513.
[19]Robert H. Estabrook, "Turkey's Reform is Half Miracle,"
Washington Post, 2 Sep. 1964, p. E6.
[20]Tutsch, op. cit., p. 44.

The growth of the Turkish economy is hampered by a lack of qualified people to perform middle-entrepreneurial, professional, and technical jobs. This situation has persisted since the 1920's, when Kemal Ataturk drove out the Greeks and other foreigners who had for centuries carried on most of the business, professional, and technological life in Turkey. Little by little the Turks are learning to do these things for themselves, and today more and more private businesses, factories, hotels, and restaurants are springing up.[21]

Turkey is relatively rich in natural resources, but to sell these resources on the world market at competitive prices requires heavy investment in machinery or a government subsidy. The same is true in the field of agriculture. To purchase the machinery with which to build a competitive economy, Turkey has gone heavily into debt to Western creditors, particularly the United States. By 1960 the total foreign debt was equal to approximately one-fifth of the gross national product. Surveys indicate Turkey cannot help incurring further deficits in foreign trade.[22] The average annual value of Turkey's exports per head of population is $12, as compared to $204 for Britain and $18 for Libya.[23]

Turkey's principal mineral resources--coal, chromium, manganese, copper, and crude oil--are relatively under-developed.

---

[21]Donna Adams Schmidt, "Turkey's New Prospects," New York Times, 23 Feb. 1965, p. 12.

[22]"Turkey," Worldmark, Vol. 4, 1963, p. 343.

[23]Geoffrey L. Lewis, "Turkey 1962-4," The World Today, Vol. 20, Dec. 1964, p. 522.

Efforts are being made to improve the iron-producing industries in northeast Turkey, but this program is hampered by the fact that the iron ore and the coal needed to process it are found at widely separated locations.

Many of the agricultural problems are caused by absentee landlordism and the inheritance laws which result in excessive fragmentation of the land into smaller and smaller units. Land reform measures to correct these problems have been proposed, but the recent political situation has prevented any action by the National Assembly.

Uncertainties about the political situation have resulted in a general hesitancy on the part of the Turks to invest in industry. Rather, they have been buying gold or investing in such things as large apartment buildings. Turkish citizens are also discouraged from investing in industry by the fact that the Constitution authorizes the government to nationalize private enterprise in the public interest.[24]

The entire situation is not black, however. Some economists see a future for Turkey and list a number of advantages which can work to her benefit in developing and strengthening her economic position. There is a well-educated elite, and some industrial development is being achieved, particularly in the sugar, cement, and chemical industries. Turkey is one of the world's largest

---

[24]Ibid.

exporters of chrome. The foundations are present, and if these are properly developed, Turkey can break the restraining barriers of economic backwardness.[25]

During the Menderes regime when credits and aid were flowing from abroad, the Turks were rather stubborn and disinclined to accept economic advice. However, there now seems to be a determined attempt to get economic planning on a sound and long-term basis. An economic planning board has been established. It is working closely with United Nations experts and has shown a willingness to seek and accept the advice of distinguished foreign economists.[26]

Although Turkey has been admitted to the European Common Market (E.C.M.) as an associate member, the association has more political than economic significance. Turkey actually receives very little economic advantage from her membership in the E.C.M., but by joining she did indicate a political choice between East and West.[27]

Turkey is a recognized, enthusiastic NATO ally, and she is proud of the fact that one of every five NATO soldiers is a Turk. This large military contribution places a very heavy strain on an already overburdened economy. Twenty-eight percent of the total budget is allocated to the Ministry of Defense for the armed

[25]"The South-East Flank of NATO," British Survey Main Series, Vol. 171, Jun. 1963, p. 19.
[26]A. N. Dragnich, "A Political and Economic Appraisal of Greece, Turkey, and Yugoslavia," Naval War College Review, Vol. XIII, Feb. 1961, p. 12.
[27]Charles Lannis, "Turkey Takes a Firm Grip on Her Bootstraps," New York Times, 1 Oct. 1964, p. 61.

forces; this figure does not include military, financial, and material aid furnished by the United States.[28] Many West-Europeans consider it an absurdity when a country with a per capita income of less that $200 maintains an army larger than those of the richest nations of Western Europe.[29]

According to Ziya Gokalp, the ideologist of Turkish nationalism, national movements go through three phases: cultural awakening, the formation of political will, and the formulation of an economic program. Assuming that Turkey has reached the third stage, it seems clear that the country is faced with a formidable task.[30]

Perhaps Turkey's current economic situation, as well as the solution to her problems, is best summed up in the following quotation from the Washington Post:

> . . . Turkey today is a half fulfilled miracle. The determination and valor of the Turks in constructing a secular Western-oriented State is almost legendary. What is still needed is the remainder of the miracle to unlock the self-generating economic growth necessary to weld a democratic nation. . . .[31]

THE ARMED FORCES

The modern Turkish armed forces date from the War of Independence (1921-1922), which marked the collapse of the Ottoman Empire and the establishment of the Republic of Turkey.

---

[28]Dr. Jurgen Weise. "Turkey and Her Armed Forces," Military Review, Vol. XLIII, May 1963, p. 83.
[29]"Turkey," The Economist, 9 Feb. 1963, p. 498.
[30]Tutsch, op. cit. p. 29.
[31]Eastabrook, op. cit., p. E6.

27

Nevertheless, Turkish military men of today draw heavily on the centuries of military traditions passed down by the Ottoman warriors: unit histories and displayed photographs of unit commanders trace the heritage of the military units well back into the 19th century.

During the latter years of the Ottoman Empire and until after World War II, the Turkish armed forces were strongly influenced by the military forces of Western Europe. This was particularly true in the case of the Army, because a large German military mission was very active in Turkish military affairs and operations throughout World War I.[32] Turkey did not participate in any military operations during World War II, but she did declare war on the Axis powers shortly before the end of the war. In 1947 the United States began a program of military and economic aid to Turkey, and since that time Turkish military tactics and organization have moved very close to the American concept.

Turkey's armed forces, with a peace-time strength of nearly half a million, are comprised of a strong army and a numerically smaller but well trained navy and air force.[33] With the principal mission of defending Turkey against external attack, the armed forces are deployed to defend the historical attack routes into Turkey.

_____

[32]Ray Brock, Ghost on Horseback, p. 71.
[33]Weise, op. cit., p. 83.

Since the spring of 1961 Turkey's armed forces have been increasingly modernized to meet the requirement of modern warfare and the new principles of management dictated by the nuclear age.[34]

Manpower

Under the constitution all males are subject to military service, and about 90 percent of the armed forces are made up by conscripts or short-term soldiers. The normal tour of obligated service is two years, but in extraordinary circumstances the term may be increased to three or four years. In actual practice the term is often three or four years for those serving in the air force and navy. The conscripts are called for duty at age 20, and it is estimated that approximately 175,000 are subject to call each year.[35]

The Turkish soldier is normally physically strong, and his peasant background enables him to suffer privation and hardship with little or no complaint. His high sense of patriotism and respect for superiors, coupled with a defiance for death, makes him a tough, stubborn, and courageous soldier. Field Marshall Lord Wavell of the British Army summed up the fighting qualities of the Turkish soldier as follows:

> As a fighter he is unlike any other soldier in the world. Even when he is wretchedly fed and miserably equipped, he will continue month after month, year after year, a

---

34"Turkey," Worldmark, Vol. 4, 1963, p. 343.
35Steinberg, op. cit., p. 1488.

dangerous foe. No set of circumstances, however depressing, appears able to diminish his dogged resistance.[36]

Upon completion of their obligated service, the conscripts return to civilian life where they remain subject to recall until age 46. The total number of reserves that could be mobilized is estimated at over two million.[37] Most reservists do not participate in active reserve training programs and would require a period of retraining before they could become fully effective. However, NATO exercises have shown that most reserve units can assemble 95 percent of their wartime strength within 24 hours.[38]

The Army is the dominant service in the Turkish armed forces. Traditionally, the Chief of the General Staff and most members of the General Staff have been army officers. It is noteworthy that both Ataturk and Inonu, as well as the present president--Gursel, were high-ranking army officers. When he was founding the First Turkish Republic, Ataturk insisted that the Chief of the General Staff be a full-fledged member of the cabinet. Later on he further emphasized the role of the military when he said:

> Whenever the Turkish nation has wanted to take a step
> up, it has always looked to the Army . . . as the leader
> of movements to achieve lofty national ideals. . . .
> When speaking of the Army, I am speaking of the

---

[36] "Turkey: Forces and Defense," <u>An Cosantoir</u>, Vol. XV, Mar. 1955, p. 137.

[37] Steinberg, <u>op. cit.</u>, p. 1488.

[38] J. F. R. Seitz, "Turkey," <u>Army Information Digest</u>, Vol. 17, Oct. 1962, p. 60.

intelligentsia of the Turkish nation who are the true
owners of this country. . . .The Turkish nation considers its army the guardian of its ideals.[39]

Turkish military officers are proud of their profession and
adhere to a rigid code of honor. They consider patriotism not
merely love of country but love for the kind of country Kemal
Ataturk tried to make. The Turks' reverence for Ataturk's teach-
ings has not diminished, and they regard the Army as the guardian
of his ideals.[40]

The Turkish Army

The Turkish Army has a strength of over 400,000 men organized
into 16 combat divisions, plus some armored brigades, administered
and controlled by three army headquarters.[41] The army units are
equipped with tanks procured from the United States and are supported
by HONEST JOHN rocket units.[42]

An enemy offensive against Turkey, either Soviet or Soviet
Bloc, would most likely be directed through Turkish Thrace toward
the Straits. Turkish First Army, with headquarters in Istanbul,
is responsible for defending the Thrace area with its nearly flat
to slightly rolling terrain. Armored units are the flexible shield
of the defense force on the Bulgarian border, which forms an arc
about 150 miles from Istanbul. The readiness of Turkish First Army

---

[39]George S. Harris, "The Role of the Military in Turkish Politics,
The Middle East Journal, Vol. 19, Winter 1965, p. 56.
[40]Claire Sterling, "Turkey's Long Interregnum," The Reporter,
Vol. 23, 1 Sep. 1960, p. 23.
[41]"Turkey," Military Review, Vol. XLIV, Sep. 1964, p. 104.
[42]The Institute for Strategic Studies, "The Military Balance
for 1962-63," Nov. 1962, p. 17.

to repel any attack coming from the Bulgarian border or across the Black Sea beaches has been repeatedly demonstrated by frequent exercises.[43]

The second most probable attack route is from Russia into the northeastern part of Turkey. The Turkish Third Army, with headquarters at Erzurum, has the mission of guarding Turkey's 360-mile border with Russia. The area is rough and mountainous, and some of the peaks are snow-covered for six months of the year. The frontier and defense lines run over difficult and well fortified mountain ranges.[44] One can safely assume that a Soviet attack in this area will be met with stiff resistance.

The Turkish Second Army, with headquarters at Konya, is responsible for the defense of Turkey's southern borders with Syria and Iraq.

The Turkish Army has excellent discipline and generally good morale. In general, units are organized, trained, and equipped in accordance with United States doctrine and procedures. But, like many other armies which depend on conscripts for manpower, the Turkish Army suffers from a shortage of career noncommissioned officers and fully qualified junior officers. Also, the army, as well as the navy and air force, suffers from equipment shortages. Secretary of Defense McNamara stressed this problem in 1964 when he said:

---

[43]Seitz, op. cit., p. 61.
[44]E. Hinterhoff, "Problems Along NATO's Flanks," Military Review, Vol. XLV, Jun. 1965, p. 54.

> . . . In almost all categories of equipment the . . .
> Turks are either seriously short of equipment or are
> operating equipment which is so old as to be of mar-
> ginal usefulness. The . . . Turks have the manpower,
> and they have the will to defend themselves; the
> problem is that the necessary equipment is missing and
> that . . . Turkey, valiant as /it is/, . . . /is/ simply
> too poor to purchase it on /its/ own account. . . .[45]

The Turkish Navy

The Turkish Navy is manned by approximately 2,100 officers
and 35,000 other ranks. The fleet consists of 9 destroyers, 10
submarines, 11 escort minesweepers, 9 coastal escorts, 6 coastal
mine layers, 16 coastal minesweepers, 6 patrol vessels, and 30
coastal craft.[46]

Although nearly three-fourths of Turkey's 6,000 miles of border
is made up of coastline, the primary mission of the Turkish Navy
is to defend the 185-mile Straits.[47] The Turkish Navy's Straits
Command handles the submarine nets which stretch across the junc-
ture of the Bosphorus and the Black Sea. Russian submarines may
pass through the Straits, but they are required to follow a pre-
scribed course and must travel by day, on the surface, and one at
a time.[48] The Turks can, and do, keep a very close tally on
Russian ships passing in and out of the Black Sea. The Turkish

---

[45]Robert S. McNamara, "The Defense of the Free World," The
Department of State Bulletin, Vol. L, 8 Jun. 1964, p. 898.

[46]Steinberg, op. cit., p. 1488.

[47]"The Shield at Thrace," The Fifteen Nations, Vol. XLV, Jun.
1965, p. 53.

[48]Seitz, op. cit., p. 60.

Navy also has a NATO role under Commander Allied Forces Mediterranean whose headquarters is at Malta.

The Turkish Air Force

The Turkish Air Force, fully jet-equipped and entirely committed to NATO, is manned by approximately 43,000 officers and men. The fighting element consists of about 300 fighter-bombers, 75 day-interceptors, and 25 all-weather fighter aircraft. The air force also has approximately 25 reconnaissance aircraft and is responsible for operation of the Nike-Ajax/Hercules air defense sites for the defense of Istanbul and the Straits. Turkish transport aircraft consist of a small number of C-130, C-54, C-47, and C-45 aircraft.[49]

The Turkish Air Force is organized into three tactical air forces (TAF). First TAF, operating in northwest Turkey, and Third TAF, operating in northeast Turkey, are concerned with conventional air-type missions: interdiction, close air support, photo reconnaissance, and air defense. The other TAF is responsible for operation of the radar warning network.[50]

---

[49]Steinberg, op. cit., p. 1489.
[50]Seitz, op. cit., p. 63.

CHAPTER 4

WHY TURKEY BECAME A NATO MEMBER

It is generally agreed that the North Atlantic Treaty
Organization (NATO) came into being because the nations of Western
Europe recognized the danger of being engulfed by communism and
realized the threat could not be countered on an individual--
country by country--basis.

In keeping with their western orientation and the expressed
desire of "Father" Ataturk to be like the West, the Turks took a
keen interest in the negotiations for the NATO alliance and the
signing of the treaty on 4 April 1949. Turkey expressed early
desires to be included in the alliance and in 1950 formally applied
for admission to NATO.[1] However, some NATO member-nations, particularly Norway and Denmark, recalled Turkey's "fence-sitting days"
of World War II and were not prepared to extend their responsibilities so far into the Middle East.

World War II left England in such a weakened condition that
she soon found that she was unable to maintain the balance of
power which had previously kept Russia from achieving her goal of
gaining control of the Turkish Straits. Consequently, shortly
after the end of World War II, England started an economic retrench-
ment and announced that she could no longer provide the economic

---

[1]Robert R. Monroe, "Geopolitics in Flux at the Turkish Straits."
Military Review, Vol. XLIII, Sep. 1963, p. 11.

and military support required to maintain western-oriented governments in Greece and Turkey.

Realizing the importance of the eastern Mediterranean to the free world, the United States embarked on a new course of foreign policy to meet the challenge. In his memoirs, President Truman explained his decision in the following words: ". . . If we were to turn our backs to the world, areas such as Greece, weakened as a result of war, would fall into the Soviet orbit without much effort on the part of the Russians. . . ."[2] Subsequently, the President of the United States unequivocally warned the Congress of the consequences of a possible refusal to help Turkey, when he said: ". . . If Greece should fall under the control of an armed minority, the effects upon its neighbor, Turkey, would be immediate and serious. Disorder and confusion might well spread throughout the Middle East."[3]

As the Turman Doctrine with its policy of containment was implemented through the application of economic and military aid, the importance and significance of Turkey and Greece became more and more apparent. The NATO planners were constantly reminded that their plans were incomplete without an "anchor" for the southern end of the defense line. In due course Greece and Turkey were admitted to NATO in March of 1952.

---

[2]Altemur Kilic, Turkey and the World, p. 136.
[3]Ibid., p. 138.

As recently as 1963 a British writer stated that the eastern Mediterranean is perhaps the most exposed part of the NATO perimeter and assessed Turkey's importance to NATO as follows:

> . . . the Dardanelles retain much of their strategic importance even in the age of missiles and nuclear weapons. The decision of the Soviet Union to concentrate on the building of submarines certainly made the Turks a welcome partner for NATO. It is highly important that those submarines be confined to the inland seas along Russia's borders as much as possible, and without control of the Straits this could not be done.[4]

General Lyman L. Lemnitzer, SACEUR, has also gone on record concerning the importance of the Turks and Turkey in the overall framework of Allied Command Europe planning. General Lemnitzer stresses the importance of interdependence and says that it would be very misleading to consider any part of Europe in isolation. In respect to Turkey, he says that the longer the Turks can resist a possible Soviet attack the more time SACEUR will have to make a choice in the wide spectrum of options within the framework of "flexible response."[5]

---

[4]"The South-Eastern Flank of NATO," British Survey Main Series, Vol. 171, Jun. 1963, p. 14.

[5]E. Hinterhoff, "Special Problems of NATO's Southern Flank," The Fifteen Nations, Vol. 10, Feb.-Mar. 1965, p. 80.

CHAPTER 5

CONCLUSIONS

If one were to evaluate the importance and significance of Turkey to NATO and the United States by comparing strengths and weaknesses on a ratio of one to one, the weaknesses would clearly outweigh the strengths. However, like most aspects of international relations and world politics, the strengths and weaknesses of a nation do not lend themselves to measurement by simple comparison.

The happenstance of geography places Turkey in a key strategic location between east and west, thereby making it inevitable that she must play a vital role in maintaining a delicate balance in world power. Turkey is important to the West, but perhaps even more important to Russia. Seizure of the Straits would enable the Russians to realize their age-old aspirations of free passage to the Mediterranean and would open the way for the spread of Soviet influence into the Middle East and North Africa.

In addition to denying Russia access to the Mediterranean, Turkey is important to NATO because by defending her homeland she threatens the left flank of a possible Soviet attack into Western Europe, or the right flank of a possible encroachment through Iran into the Middle East. Turkey also provides the "anchor" for the southern flank of NATO's defense line and has many potential bases for possible counteroffensive operations against the Soviet Bloc.

Next to strategical and geographical considerations, Turkey's greatest strength lies in the character of her soldiers. The

Turks are rugged, capable fighters whose deep belief in NATO is exceeded only by their hatred of communism and suspicion of the Russians.

Turkey's economic situation is critical, and there are no indications that it can be improved materially without massive outside aid. Turkey's contribution, as well as her overall value, to NATO will continue to be limited by this shortcoming.

The "anchor" for the southern flank of NATO has been severely weakened by the Turkish-Greek feud over Cyprus. The roots of this dispute are age-old and have many emotional undertones; therefore, a solution will require much patience and skillful diplomatic effort. Nevertheless, since continuance of the dispute can only result in more damage to the NATO Alliance and further gains for the Soviets, it is imperative that the NATO members make a maximum effort for an early solution to this problem.

Although there have been instances of anti-American feeling, actions by individual Turkish citizens and repeated statements by responsible government officials show that Turkey retains a strong faith in NATO. In fact, it seems apparent that most Turks see more to NATO than military and economic aid. NATO provides a practical means of achieving the western status and position which Ataturk said Turkey must have. This fact, plus the centuries-old conflict of interest with Russia, leaves little doubt that Turkey will continue her ties to the West, specifically NATO.

It is concluded therefore that the problem is not simply a question of "what does NATO gain from having Turkey in the alliance," but rather "what does NATO lose if Turkey becomes neutralist or joins the Soviet Bloc?"

It is clear beyond reasonable doubt that Turkey is essential to NATO. She will continue to support the cause of freedom to the full extent of her capabilities, but she is greatly hampered by her meager economic and industrial development and by the abject poverty of the great majority of her people. The current trend seems to be for the wealthier nations to concentrate on finding ways and means of helping underdeveloped countries. It is my firm conviction that a higher priority should be given to helping this underdeveloped but faithful and indispensable NATO ally.

NORMAN R. HALEY
Lt. Col.   Arty

BIBLIOGRAPHY

1. Abigadol, Meryem. "Turkish Bridgehead." <u>NATO Letter</u>, Vol. 8, May 1960, pp. 2-5.

2. Alpan, Cihad. "The Strategic Importance of Turkey." <u>NATO Letter</u>, Vol. 10, Feb. 1962, pp. 7-11.

3. Birge, John K. <u>A Guide to Turkish Area Study</u>. Richmond: William Byrd Press, 1949. (DR417 B5)

    (An excellent reference for material published prior to 1945.)

4. Brock, Ray. <u>Ghost on Horseback: The Incredible Ataturk</u>. New York: Duell, Sloan, and Pearce, 1954. (DR592 K4B7)

    (Excellent background on the life of Ataturk and his fight to build a new Turkey.)

5. Bullard, Sir Reader, ed. <u>The Middle East</u>. London: Oxford University Press, 1958, pp. 488-531. (DS49 R87)

    (This book contains data and information on the Turkish people, economy, and politics.)

6. Cressey, George B. <u>Crossroads: Land and Life in Southwest Asia</u>. Chicago: J. B. Lippincott Co., 1960. (DS49.7 C7)

7. Desbocquets, Claude. "Turkey and Global Strategy." <u>Military Review</u>, Vol. XLI, Jun. 1961, pp. 60-67.

8. Dinsdale, Walter G. "Turkey Faces West and East." <u>The Fifteen Nations</u>, Vol. 12, Jan. 1960, pp. 114-119.

    (A Canadian view of present day Turkey and its importance to NATO.)

9. Dragnich, A. N. "A Political and Economic Appraisal of Greece, Turkey, and Yugoslavia." <u>Naval War College Review</u>, Vol. XII, Feb. 1961, pp. 1-20.

10. Eren, Nuri. "Turkey: Problems, Policies, Parties." <u>Foreign Affairs</u>, Vol. 40, Oct. 1961, pp. 95-104.

    (A review of Turkey's internal situation in mid-1961, and indications of possible future happenings.)

11. Estabrook, Robert H. "Turkey's Reform Is Half Miracle." <u>Washington Post</u>, 2 Sep. 1964, p. E6.

12. Harris, George S. "The Role of Military in Turkish Politics." The Middle East Journal, Vol. 19, Winter 1965, pp. 54-66.

13. Hessler, William H. "Turkey-Russia's Gift to NATO." The Reporter, Vol. 5, 2 Oct. 1951, pp. 14-16.

    (A review of Turkey's war potential and role in Western defenses.)

14. Hinterhoff, E. "Problems Along NATO's Flanks." Military Review, Vol. XLV, Jun. 1965, pp. 48-55.

15. Hinterhoff, E. "Special Problems of NATO's Southern Flank." The Fifteen Nations, Vol. 10, Feb.-Mar. 1965, pp. 77-82.

    (An informative article of considerable value in the preparation of this study.)

16. Hinterhoff, E. "The Strategic Importance of Turkey." Asian Review, Vol. LV, Jan. 1959, pp. 53-57.

17. Hurewitz, J. C. Diplomacy in the Middle East--A Documentary Record 1914-1956. Princeton: D. Van Nostrand Co., Inc., 1956. (JX1568.5 H9)

    (An excellent reference containing verbatum treaties concerning diplomacy in the Middle East.)

18. Karpat, Kemal H. "Recent Political Developments in Turkey and Their Social Background." International Affairs, Vol. 38, Jul. 1962, pp. 304-324.

    (A discussion of the social and political situations in Turkey with emphasis on the period immediately following the coup of 1960; provided excellent background information for the preparation of this study.)

19. Karpat, Kemal H. Turkey's Politics. Princeton: Princeton University Press, 1959. (JN9798 A1K3)

    (Primary source for preparation of this study.)

20. Kilic, Altemur. Turkey and the World. Washington: Public Affairs Press, 1959. (DR590 K5)

    (An interesting and informative review of recent Turkish history from the viewpoint of a Turkish citizen who has lived in the United States.)

21. Kuhn, Ferdinand. "Where Turk and Russian Meet." National Geographic Magazine, Vol. CI, Jun. 1952, pp. 743-766.

(A discussion of the military and sociological conditions along the Turkish-Soviet border.)

22. Lanuis, Charles. "Turkey Takes a Firm New Grip on Her Economic Bootstraps." New York Times, 1 Oct. 1964, p. 61.

23. Lens, Sidney. "Turkey's Internal Crisis." The Commonweal, Vol. LXXX, 18 Sep. 1964, pp. 629-631.

   (This article considers the Cyprus crisis from the standpoint of its impact on Turkey's internal politics.)

24. Lewis, Bernard. The Emergence of Modern Turkey. London: Oxford University Press, 1961. (DR440 L45)

   (Excellent coverage of Turkish history from the end of the Ottoman Empire through the 1950's.)

25. Lewis, Geoffrey. Turkey. London: Ernest Benn Limited, 1960. (DR477 L4)

   (This interesting and well-written book gives excellent coverage on the history, people, culture, and economy of modern Turkey; a primary reference for the preparation of this study.)

26. Lewis, Geoffrey. "Turkey, 1962-4." The World Today, Vol. 20, Dec. 1964, pp. 517-522.

   (A summary of the political and economic situations as they existed in Turkey in 1964.)

27. Luman, H. Long, ed. The World Almanac. New York: World-Telegram, 1966, pp. 639-640.

28. McGhee, George C. "Turkey Joins the West." Foreign Affairs, Vol. 32, Jul. 1964, pp. 617-630.

   (A summary of Turkey's position in the East-West struggle; a primary reference for the preparation of this study.)

29. McNamara, Robert S. "The Defense of the Free World." The Department of State Bulletin, Vol. L, 8 Jun. 1964, pp. 893-899.

30. Monroe, Robert R. "Geopolitics in Flux at the Turkish Straits." Military Review, Vol. XLIII, Sep. 1963, pp. 3-15.

   (This article reviews the reasons for the strategic importance of Turkey; a valuable reference for the preparation of this study.)

31. North Atlantic Treaty Organization. <u>NATO: Facts About the North Atlantic Treaty Organization</u>. Paris: 1962. (JX1987 A41 A124)

32. Peretz, Don. <u>The Middle East Today</u>. New York: Holt, Rinehardt, and Winston, Inc., 1964. (DS63 P4)

33. Perlman, Moshe. "Turkey on the Eve of 1961." <u>Middle Eastern Affairs</u>, Vol. 12, Jan. 1961, pp. 6-7.

    (A review of the actions taken by General Gursel and the Committee of National Union from the time of the coup in May 1960 until the end of the year.)

34. Pipinelis, Panayotis. "The Greco-Turkish Feud Revived." <u>Foreign Affairs</u>, Vol. 37, Jan. 1959, pp. 306-316.

35. Sachs, Moshe Y., ed. <u>Worldmark Encyclopedia of the Nations Asia and Australia</u>. Chicago: 1963, pp. 339-350.

36. Sadok, Necmeddin. "Turkey Faces the Soviets." <u>Foreign Affairs</u>, Vol. 27, Apr. 1949, pp. 449-461.

37. Schmidt, Donna Adams. "Turkey's New Prospects." <u>New York Times</u>, 23 Feb. 1965, p. 12.

38. Seitz, J. F. R. "Turkey." <u>Army Information Digest</u>, Vol. 17, Oct. 1962, pp. 59-63.

    (An interesting and informative article on the organization and missions of the Turkish armed forces; a valuable reference for the preparation of this study.)

39. Shotwell, James T. <u>Turkey at the Straits</u>. New York: Macmillan, 1940. (DR741 B7S45)

    (This book reviews the history of the Turkish Straits with emphasis on the strategic importance, the struggles for control, and the various treaties concerning its use.)

40. Steinberg, S. H., ed. <u>The Statesman's Yearbook</u>. New York: St. Martin's Press, 1965, pp. 1482-1495. (JA51 S75)

41. Sterling, Claire. "Turkey's Long Interregnum." <u>The Reporter</u>, Vol. 23, 1 Sep. 1960, p. 25.

    (Excellent coverage on the 1960 military coup.)

42. Storke, Harry P. "NATO's Right Flank 'Anchor'." <u>The Fifteen Nations</u>, Vol. 6, Oct.-Nov. 1961, pp. 67-71.

43. Sulzberger, C. L. "Foreign Affairs: When Armies Enter Politics." New York Times, 13 Feb. 1966, p. E12.

44. Szylrowicz, Joseph S. "The Political Dynamics of Rural Turkey." The Middle East Journal, Vol. 16, Autumn 1962, pp. 430-442.

   (This article stresses the important role the Turkish peasant will play in determining the future of Turkey.)

45. The Institute for Strategic Studies, The Military Balance, 1962-1963. London: 1962. (UA15 I5)

46. "The Shield at Thrace." The Fifteen Nations, Vol. 6, Aug.-Sep. 1961, pp. 50-54.

47. "The South-Eastern Flank of NATO." British Survey Main Series, Vol. 171, Jun. 1963, pp. 11-19.

48. "Turkey." Military Review, Vol. XLIV, Sep. 1964, p. 104.

   (Unclassified estimate of the composition of Turkey's armed forces.)

49. Turkish Information Office. Turkey's Foreign Policy--1958. Ankara: 1958. (JX1568 A3)

   (Translation of a speech by Foreign Minister Zorlu made on the floor of the Turkish Parliament on 25 Feb. 1958.)

50. "Turkey: Forces and Defence." An Cosantoir, The Irish Defence Journal, Vol. XV, Mar. 1955, pp. 133-141.

51. "Turkey--Rampart in the Middle East." Army Information Digest, Vol. 7, May 1952, pp. 34-48.

   (A short history of the Turkish military establishment and foreign relations from early nineteenth century to 1950.)

52. Tutsch, Hans E. From Ankara to Marrakesh. London: George Allen and Unwin, Limited, 1964. (DS63 T8)

53. Von Mikusch, Dagobert. Mustafa Kemal. London: William Heinemann, Limited, 1931. (DR592 K4M55)

   (A biography of Ataturk with excellent coverage of the last days of the Ottoman Empire.)

54. Weiker, Walter F. The Turkish Revolution 1960-1961. Washington: TheBrookings Institute, 1963. (DR590 W4)

(This book provides background and detail on the 1960 coup, and covers the new constitution and the development of the multiparty system in Turkey. An excellent summary of recent political events and their impact on Turkey.)

55. Weise, Dr. Jurgen. "Turkey and Her Armed Forces." Military Review, Vol. XLIII, May 1963, pp. 80-86.

(Excellent coverage of the current status and organization of the Turkish armed forces.)

www.ingramcontent.com/pod-product-compliance
Lightning Source LLC
Chambersburg PA
CBHW081427280526
45788CB00009B/3245